Macbeth, King of Scotland

by David Orme

adapted from the play by William Shakespeare

GW00728118

The Cast: Macbeth
                  Lady Macbeth
                  Duncan, the King
                  Macolm and Donalbain, his sons
                  Macduff and Banquo, Scottish noblemen
                  Three Witches
                  Siward, a brave soldier
                  Macbeth's Servant
                  A Murderer
                  A Doctor
                  Scottish Lords

*Act 1 Scene 1: A bleak Moor in Scotland. A great battle
has been fought.*

Enter three Witches

Witch 1   When shall we three meet again?
                  In thunder, lightning or in rain?

Witch 2   When the hurley-burley's done,
                  when the battle's lost or won.

Sound of a drum

Witch 3   A drum, a drum! Macbeth doth come.

All Witches   Weird sisters, hand in hand
                  Wandering over sea and land,
                  Thus do go, about, about.

Witch 1	Peace! The spell is cast

Enter Macbeth and Banquo

Macbeth	I have never seen so foul a day, Banquo. Yet what a victory we have won!
Banquo	The enemy are destroyed, but now we're lost in this fog!
Macbeth	Maybe those three weird-looking old women know where we are.
Witch 1	Hail, Macbeth!
Witch 2	Hail, Macbeth, Thane of Cawdor!
Witch 3	Hail Macbeth, who will be King!
Macbeth	I'm not the Thane of Cawdor! And what do you mean, I will be King! Come on, speak up!
Banquo	They've vanished into the air like bubbles! What strange creatures they were!
Macbeth	And a strange message, too.

Enter Macduff

Macbeth	What news, Macduff?

Macduff   Macbeth! I have news for you from King
Duncan. You fought bravely in battle, and
he has heard of your success. He has
given you a great honour!

Banquo   He certainly deserves it!

Macbeth   What is it, Macduff?

Macduff   You know that the Thane of Cawdor was a
traitor to the King? The King has executed
him and given you his title. He has made
you Thane of Cawdor!

Macbeth   *(quietly to himself)* Thane of Cawdor –
that's what the old women said. They got
that right. Maybe they will be right about me
being King, too!

Act 1 Scene 2: *Dunsinane Castle, the home of Macbeth.*

Enter Lady Macbeth, with a letter

Lady Macbeth My husband has sent me a letter. *(reading it)*
My dear wife,

The battle went well and the Norwegians are defeated. Afterwards Banquo and I met three strange women. They seemed to know who I was! They called me 'Macbeth, Thane of Cawdor' and 'Macbeth, who will be King'. I was amazed! I wanted to ask them more questions, but they just vanished!

Then, an even more amazing thing happened. Macduff arrived, and told me that the King had made me Thane of Cawdor! How could the three women know that? They also said that I would be King. They were right about the first thing, so maybe they will be right about that as well!

Don't tell anyone about this. I will be home soon.

From your loving husband,
Macbeth.

King of Scotland! That means I would be Queen!

Enter A Servant

Servant   My Lady, the King is coming here tonight.

Lady Macbeth The King! How do you know?

Servant   Our Thane, Macbeth, sent a servant on ahead with the news. They will be arriving soon!

Exit Servant

Lady Macbeth The King is sleeping here. It will be his last night on earth! Tonight he will die. Macbeth will be King, and I will be Queen!

Enter Macbeth

Macbeth   My dearest wife, King Duncan is coming.

Lady Macbeth And when will he leave?

Macbeth   Tomorrow.

Lady Macbeth He will never see tomorrow! When the King comes, treat him well and put him at his ease. Tonight, he will die, so make sure he doesn't suspect anything!

Act 2 Scene 1: *That night – Dunsinane Castle.*

Enter King Duncan, Macbeth and Lady Macbeth

King Duncan My dear friends! Thanks you very much for your kindness! You have made me very welcome at your castle. I am tired now and I will go to bed. I must be up and away early in the morning.

Macbeth Goodnight, your majesty. And thank you for making me Thane of Cawdor!

Lady Macbeth Sleep well, your majesty...

Exit Duncan

Macbeth I can't go through with this business! After all, I am a member of the King's family, and he is a guest in my house! Duncan is a fine king, and has given me a great honour. To kill him would be a great sin.

Lady Macbeth If you hadn't wanted to be King, you wouldn't have told me about the three weird women. I thought you were brave. All I hear from you is weakness! You are an ambitious man. Now show it with your actions! Are you a man, or just a coward?

Macbeth   But what if something went wrong and we were found out?

Lady Macbeth Then we would suffer for it! But it won't go wrong. Duncan has two bodyguards, but I will give them so much wine that they will be completely drunk. They won't know what is going on. When they are all asleep, take your dagger and kill him!

Macbeth   What a wife you are! You have given me courage. I will do it!

Exit Lady Macbeth

Enter Banquo

Macbeth   Good evening, friend Banquo.

Banquo   Greetings, Macbeth. I have been thinking about the three weird women we saw on the heath. Have you thought any more about what they said?

Macbeth   Oh, them! No, I had forgotten all about it! I'm really tired now, Banquo. I'm off to bed. Good night!

Banquo   Goodnight, Macbeth!

Act 2 Scene 2: *Later that night.*

Enter Macbeth and servant

Macbeth   Go and tell my wife to ring the bell when my drink is ready.

Servant   Yes, my lord.

Exit servant

Macbeth   *(holding a dagger)* Here is the dagger, ready to do the deed. Everyone is asleep, and everything is working out as we planned it. *(a bell rings)* All is ready, she has rung the bell. Tomorrow will I be King, or will I be in hell?

Macbeth exits. There is a scream, then silence. An owl hoots. Macbeth comes back. Lady Macbeth enters.

Macbeth   I have done it. I have killed Duncan, and his bodyguards. Did you hear a noise?

Lady Macbeth I heard the owl scream.

Macbeth   Look at my hands! They are covered in blood.

Lady Macbeth Get some water and wash them before someone sees them!

9

Macbeth   I thought I heard a voice, speaking to me
                  just after I killed them.

Lady Macbeth What did it say?

Macbeth   It said "No sleep for Macbeth! Macbeth will
                  never sleep again!"

Lady Macbeth Pull yourself together! You are just
                  imagining things! Now, why did you bring
                  the dagger back with you? You should have
                  left it there. Hurry up. Wash your hands,
                  and no-one will know it was us!

Act 3 Scene 1: *Dunsinane Castle, next morning.*

Enter Macduff and Macbeth

Macduff   Has the King woken up yet? He said he was going to leave early.

Macbeth   Not yet. I'll just go and wake him up.

Macbeth leaves. He gives a terrible cry, then rushes on again

Macbeth   The King is dead! Stabbed to death by his own bodyguards, the traitors! I was so angry, I have killed both of them in my rage!

Enter Lady Macbeth followed by a servant

Lady Macbeth What has happened? Why are you shouting?

Macduff   The King has been murdered!

Lady Macbeth What, in our house? Who has done this dreadful thing?

Macbeth   His own bodyguards. The daggers were still in their hands, red with the King's blood. I have killed both of them!

Macduff   *(to the Servant)* Hey, you there! Go and wake up the King's sons and bring them here. Someone must break the news to them.

Exit Servant

Enter the King's sons, Malcolm and Donalbain

Malcolm   What has happened? What's going on?

Macbeth   I have terrible news. Your father has been murdered.

Lady Macbeth By his bodyguards.

Macbeth   Yes, by his bodyguards.

Lady Macbeth Let us go and pray by the body.

Exit everyone except Malcolm and Donalbain.

Donalbain   Our father, dead! And his bodyguards seemed so loyal to him!

Malcolm   They were loyal to him! I would have trusted them with my life. Did you see how nervous Macbeth looked? I am sure he was the one who murdered our father. My guess is, that wife of his put him up to it.

Donalbain   But why should he do such a thing?

Malcolm   After us, he is the next King!

Donalbain   But that means...

Malcolm   Yes, that means we're next! Come on Donalbain. Let's head for England. We're not strong enough to fight Macbeth yet. But one day we will be – and we'll get our revenge!

Enter Banquo and Macduff

Banquo   So who did murder the King?

Macduff   His bodyguards. Now Malcolm and Donalbain have fled. That looks suspicious... maybe they are behind it!

Banquo   So who will be King now?

Macduff   Macbeth, of course.

Exit Macduff

Banquo   So now Macbeth has it all – Cawdor and the crown! The three old women were right – but was it chance, or did Macbeth make it happen?

Exit Banquo

Enter Macbeth with a Murderer

Macbeth   You are to kill Banquo. And make sure you get the right person, or you're the one who will end up dead!

Murderer   Don't worry, your majesty, I won't make a mistake.

Exit Murderer

Macbeth   There are enemies all round me. I must be careful!

Act 3 Scene 2: *Dunsinane Castle. There is a great feast to celebrate Macbeth being crowned King.*

Macbeth Welcome, Lords. Welcome to my castle.

Lords Greetings, your majesty.

Lady Macbeth Eat and drink, my lords. There is plenty for everyone.

Enter Murderer. He whispers into Macbeth's ear

Murderer That little job you asked me to do, your majesty. It's done!

Macbeth Good. Don't tell me about it now though, people will get suspicious.

Murderer What about my money?

Macbeth Later!

Exit Murderer

Macbeth *(walking towards his throne)* Let the feast begin!

Enter Banquo's ghost. He sits on Macbeth's throne.

Macbeth Who is that? Who is sitting on my throne?

15

Lady Macbeth What do you mean? There's no-one there at all.

Macbeth Yes there is, and I know that face. He's come back to haunt me!

First Lord What's the matter?

Second Lord Your majesty, are you ill?

Third Lord He's very pale. He looks as if he's seen a ghost!

Lady Macbeth Pull yourself together! What will they all think of their new King?

Exit Banquo's ghost

Macbeth It's gone now. Sorry about that, everyone. It's just my imagination. I've been under a lot of strain recently.

Enter the ghost

Macbeth It's back! Don't you glare, and shake your head at me!

Lady Macbeth Don't worry, my lords. He has these strange fits sometimes. He'll be all right in a minute.

16

First Lord   What can you see, your majesty?

Lady Macbeth Don't ask him questions, it just makes him worse. I'm sorry, my lords, but the feast is over. The King needs a lie down.

Exit Lords

Macbeth   I knew it! We are doomed. Everything is going wrong. Macduff refused to come to the feast, then I saw… it was terrible! I will go and find the three weird sisters once more. Maybe they can tell me what the future holds for me!

Act 4 Scene 1: *A bleak moor.*

Enter the three Witches

Witch 1   Round about the cauldron go,
                In it poisoned innards throw,

Witch 2   Fillet of a poisonous snake,
                In the cauldron boil and bake,

Witch 3   Eye of newt and toe of frog,
                Hair of bat and tongue of dog,

Witch 1   Dragon's scales and hornet's stings,
                Lizard's legs and owlet's wings,

All Witches For a charm of powerful trouble
                Let the cauldron boil and bubble.
                Double, double, toil and trouble,
                Fire burn, and cauldron bubble.

Enter Macbeth

Macbeth   How now, you secret hags, what are you
                doing?

All Witches Something wicked that has no name.

Macbeth   I command you to answer my questions.

Witch 1	Speak.
Macbeth	Tell me whether…
Witch 2	Say no more. We already know your question.
Witch 3	Beware Macduff! He is your enemy.
Macbeth	I thought so! Now, what will happen to me?
Witch 1	No man born of a woman can harm you.
Macbeth	Good news! Now my last question. Will I ever be defeated?
Witch 2	Not until Birnam wood reaches your castle!
Macbeth	Even better news! How can a forest pull up its roots and come to my castle? That's impossible! They must mean that I will never be defeated. Now, just a few more things I need to know…
Witch 1	No more questions! We have one more thing to show you.

All Witches   Double, double, toil and trouble,
Fire burn and cauldron bubble,
Now we'll have our little joke;
You'll see strange shapes form
In the smoke!
Livers sizzle! fingers roast!
What is this?

Macbeth   It's Banquo's ghost!

Exit Macbeth in a hurry

Act 4 Scene 2: *In Birnam wood, a few miles from Dunsinane Castle.*

Enter Malcolm, Donalbain and Macduff

Malcolm Macduff, I have terrible news for you. I've just had a report from one of my messengers. Your entire family has been murdered.

Macduff My whole family? What? My wife, and all my children?

Malcolm I am afraid that that is what the messenger said.

Macduff My wife! My poor children! Who could have done such a terrible thing?

Donalbain Can't you guess who it was?

Macduff Of course! Macbeth ordered it, that evil Macbeth!

Donalbain It was Macbeth who killed our father so that he could become King. Macbeth and that wicked wife of his planned it all.

Malcolm It was Macbeth that had Banquo murdered too.

21

Donalbain	Turn your sad thoughts to revenge, Macduff. We have a loyal army here. Many soldiers from England are fighting on our side. We will march on Dunsinane Castle. When we get there, you will be the one to kill Macbeth!
Macduff	The castle is well guarded. They will see us coming. It will be very difficult to attack it across open ground.
Donalbain	That's very true. If only there was a way to get there without being seen.
Malcolm	I know an old trick! We will tell every soldier to cut down a branch of a tree, and hold it in front of him. The army will be hidden.
Donalbain	A very good idea, brother. It will make you King tomorrow! Now where is that brave young captain, Siward?
Siward	I am here, sir.
Donalbain	You have shown how brave you are. I want you to lead the attack on the castle.
Siward	Thank you for the great honour. I won't let you down. Come on men. Revenge or death!

Act 5 Scene 1: *At Dunsinane Castle.*

Enter Macbeth, with a Doctor

Macbeth   Doctor, is there nothing you can do to cure my wife?

Doctor   I am sorry, your majesty, I do not have the skill.

Macbeth   What is wrong with her?

Doctor   She will not speak to anyone, she only talks to herself, and pretends to wash her hands. She washes them over and over again!

Macbeth   What does she say?

Doctor   She says 'Out, damned spot, out! Will my hands never be clean? Who would have thought the old man had so much blood in him?'

Macbeth   I can't imagine what she means by that. Keep me informed of how things are going, doctor.

Enter Servant

Macbeth   What news?

Servant   There are reports of a huge English army, your majesty. They are heading this way.

Macbeth   Rubbish! I don't believe a word of it! No one would dare. Get out, you fool!

Exit Servant

Macbeth   Let them all come! No army can defeat me, the witches told me! What was it they said? I won't be defeated until Birnam Wood comes to Dunsinane! Well, that's not going to happen!

There is a cry off stage, enter the Doctor

Macbeth   What is it?

Doctor   I'm afraid that your wife has just died.

Macbeth   My wife! Snuffed out, just like a candle!

Enter Servant

Servant   There is more news, your majesty.

Macbeth   Get out! I don't want to hear anything!

Servant   You must hear this, your majesty. I was
looking out over the castle walls - and I saw
moving trees!

Macbeth   What do you mean?

Servant   Birnam Wood, your majesty! It was moving
towards the castle!

Act 5 Scene 2: *Outside Dunsinane Castle.*

Enter Macbeth

Macbeth   The castle is surrounded. I won't try and escape. After all I cannot be killed by anyone here. No man of woman born, the witches said. Everyone is born of a woman! That means no-one can kill me!

Enter Siward

Siward   What is your name?

Macbeth   My name is Macbeth, King of Scotland.

Siward   With my sword I will show that you are not fit to hold such a title!

They fight, and Siward is killed by Macbeth

Macbeth   You were born of a woman! I can laugh at swords; no-one can kill me!

Enter Macduff

Macduff   Come on, you dog! I will have my revenge for what you did to my family.

Macbeth   I have nothing to say to you. Come and fight!

They fight

Macbeth   You see, you cannot kill me, Macduff. I have a charmed life. I cannot be killed by anyone born of a woman.

Macduff   Then prepare to die, Macbeth! My mother died just before the moment of my birth. She was not a woman when I was born — she was dead!

Macbeth   Your words bring fear to my heart. I won't fight with you.

Macduff   Then surrender, you coward!

Macbeth   I am not a coward! Fight on, Macduff!

They fight, and Macbeth is killed. Enter Malcolm and Donalbain

Donalbain   Is the traitor dead?

Macduff   He is dead.

Malcolm   So there the traitor lies; Macduff has struck him down.
(to Macduff) For this you'll be an earl; and I will wear the crown!

The End